FIRST SCIENCE LIBRARY
On the Move

- 15 EASY-TO-FOLLOW EXPERIMENTS FOR LEARNING FUN
- FIND OUT ABOUT THINGS THAT GO – INCLUDING YOU!

WENDY MADGWICK

ARMADILLO

This edition is published by Armadillo,
an imprint of Anness Publishing Ltd,
108 Great Russell Street, London WC1B 3NA; info@anness.com

www.annesspublishing.com

If you like the images in this book and would like to investigate using them for publishing, promotions or advertising, please visit our website www.practicalpictures.com for more information.

Publisher: Joanna Lorenz
Designer: Anita Ruddell
Illustrations: Catherine Ward/Simon Girling Associates
Photographers: Andrew Sydenham, with Paul Forrester
    (page 11 bottom left)
Many thanks to JD, Kaori, Kondwani, Liuzayani,
    Poppy and Shinnosuke for appearing
    in the book
Production Controller: Mai-Ling Collyer

PUBLISHER'S NOTE
Although the advice and information in this book are believed to be accurate and true at the time of going to press, neither the authors nor the publisher can accept any legal responsibility or liability for any errors or omissions that may have been made nor for any inaccuracies nor for any loss, harm or injury that comes about from following instructions or advice in this book.

Words that appear in **bold** in the text are explained in the glossary on page 32.

Manufacturer: Anness Publishing Ltd,
108 Great Russell Street,
London WC1B 3NA, England
For Product Tracking go to:
www.annesspublishing.com/tracking
Batch: 7012-22871-1127

Contents

Looking at movement and forces

Objects cannot move by themselves. They need a **force** to push or pull them. This book has lots of fun activities to help you find out about movement and forces.

Here are some simple rules you should follow before doing an activity.

- Always tell a grown-up what you are doing. Ask him or her if you can do the activity.
- Always read through the activity before you start. Collect all the materials you will need and put them on a tray.
- Make sure you have enough space to set up your activity.
- Follow the steps carefully.
- Watch what happens carefully.
- Keep a notebook. Draw pictures or write down what you did and what happened.
- Always clear up when you have finished, and wash your hands.

▶ These skydivers are pulled towards the ground by **gravity**. Find out about this super strong force on page 6.

Going down

All objects have a force called gravity around them. This pulls other objects towards them. Big objects have more pulling power than small ones. The Earth is so big that its gravity pulls objects down to it.

Fast or slow?

You will need: a light plastic brick and a wooden brick of the same size, tray.

Collect a light plastic brick and a heavy wooden brick of the same size. Put a tray on the floor in front of you. Stand with your arms at the same level. Let go of the bricks at the same time. Which one hits the tray first?

Both bricks hit the tray at the same time. Gravity pulls the bricks down to Earth at the same speed.

Thud!

When an object falls, it hits the ground with force. Is the force bigger the further an object falls? Let's find out.

You will need: plastic bowl, wet sand, strip of thin cardboard, ruler, marble, pencil and paper.

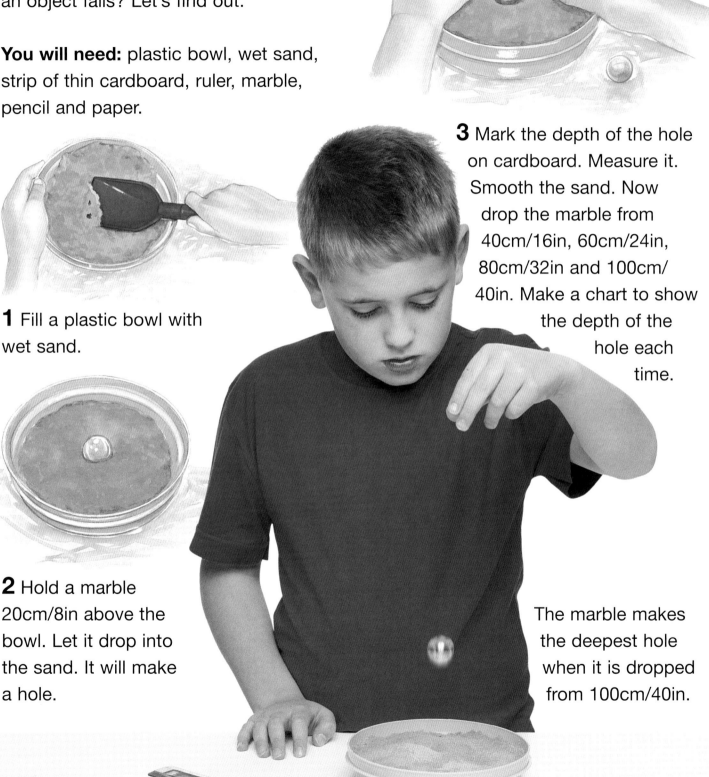

1 Fill a plastic bowl with wet sand.

2 Hold a marble 20cm/8in above the bowl. Let it drop into the sand. It will make a hole.

3 Mark the depth of the hole on cardboard. Measure it. Smooth the sand. Now drop the marble from 40cm/16in, 60cm/24in, 80cm/32in and 100cm/40in. Make a chart to show the depth of the hole each time.

The marble makes the deepest hole when it is dropped from 100cm/40in.

7

Ready, steady, go!

Objects won't move on their own. You have to apply a force to make them move. You can do this by pulling or pushing an object.

> **You will need:** toy truck, rubber band, ruler, toy bricks, cardboard tube, three or four big books, golf ball.

Pulling power

1 Tie a rubber band to an empty toy truck. Put a ruler on the floor beside the truck.

2 Pull the band until the truck starts to move. How far has the band stretched?

3 Now fill the truck with toy bricks. Pull the band again.

Did the band stretch more or less with the full truck?

The band stretched more with the full truck. The longer the band, the harder you are pulling it. Heavier objects need more force to start them moving.

8

Push off!

1 Rest a cardboard tube against some big books to form a steep slope. Put a toy truck at the end of the tube.

3 Fill the truck with toy bricks. Repeat step 2. How far does the truck roll this time? Which truck rolls further? The empty truck should roll further.

2 Put a ruler beside the truck. Roll a golf ball down the tube to hit the truck. Measure how far the truck moves.

Let's slide

Two surfaces rubbing together make a force called **friction**. Smooth things make less friction than rough things.

▲ It is easy to slide down snowy surfaces or over ice. Both surfaces are smooth and make little friction.

Feeling friction

When you rub your hands together they get warm. This heat is caused by friction.

Super sliders

Let's see what things slide best.

You will need: wooden brick, ice cube, small rock, eraser, wooden board.

1 Place a wooden brick, a small rock, an ice cube and an eraser at one edge of a wooden board.

2 Slowly raise the board until the objects start to slide. Which one starts to slide first? Which ones slide most easily?

The ice cube should move first. The smooth things will move most easily.

Smooth objects move more easily because there is little friction between them and the wood.

◀ We use oil or grease to stop moving parts rubbing against each other. This reduces friction and helps the parts move more easily.

11

Slow down!

Friction tries to stop things sliding over one another. It slows things down.

▲ This tractor has large knobbly tyres to grip the slippery, wet soil.

Grip the ground

Try running in slippery socks. Now try in trainers (sneakers). Which is easier?

The trainers help you to run. There is friction between the soles of your trainers and the ground. This helps you grip the ground. It stops you from slipping over when you run.

Getting a grip

You will need: smooth wooden board, two large books, plastic brick, a watch with a second   hand, sandpaper, woollen fabric, foam rubber, cotton fabric, pencil and paper.

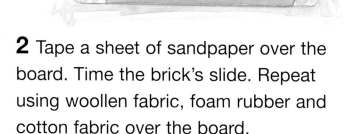

2 Tape a sheet of sandpaper over the board. Time the brick's slide. Repeat using woollen fabric, foam rubber and cotton fabric over the board.

1 Rest a smooth wooden board against two large books to make a slope. Put a plastic brick at the top. Let it go. Time how long the brick takes to reach the bottom.

Make a chart of your results. Which surfaces slow down the brick most? Rough surfaces have the greatest friction. They have the best grip and slow down the brick most.

13

Rolling along

Some things are hard to move. Slopes and wheels can make them easier to move.

Super slope

You will need: string, toy car, toy bucket, small bricks, some large books, piece of cardboard.

1 Tie a long piece of string to a toy car. Tie the other end to the handle of a toy bucket.

2 Place the car and bucket over a pile of books as shown. Put toy bricks in the bucket. How many bricks are needed to lift the car to the top?

3 Put a piece of cardboard against the books to make a slope. How many bricks are needed to pull the car up the slope? It should take fewer bricks to pull the car up the slope.

Free wheeling

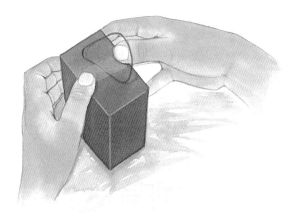

You will need: small rubber band, small cardboard box, ruler, two straws, four empty cotton reels, non-hardening clay. Ask a grown-up to help.

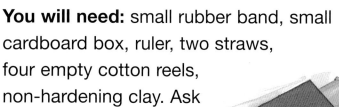

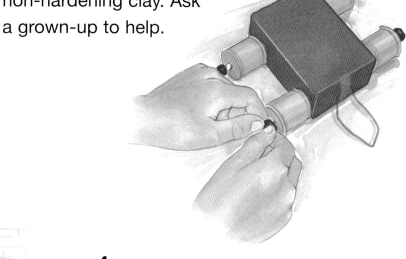

1 Tape a small rubber band to a small box.

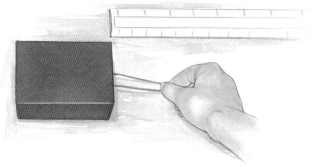

2 Put a ruler on the floor beside the box. Pull the rubber band until the box starts to move. Measure how far the band stretches.

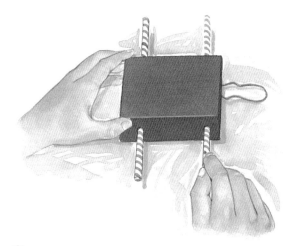

3 Ask a grown-up to make two holes in both sides of the box. Push straws through the holes.

4 Push a cotton reel on to each end of both straws. Fix a ball of clay to all four ends.

5 Move the wheeled box by pulling the band. Does the band stretch more or less?

The band should stretch less. It takes less force to move the wheeled box.

Pulley power

Pulleys are special kinds of wheels.
They help to lift heavy loads.

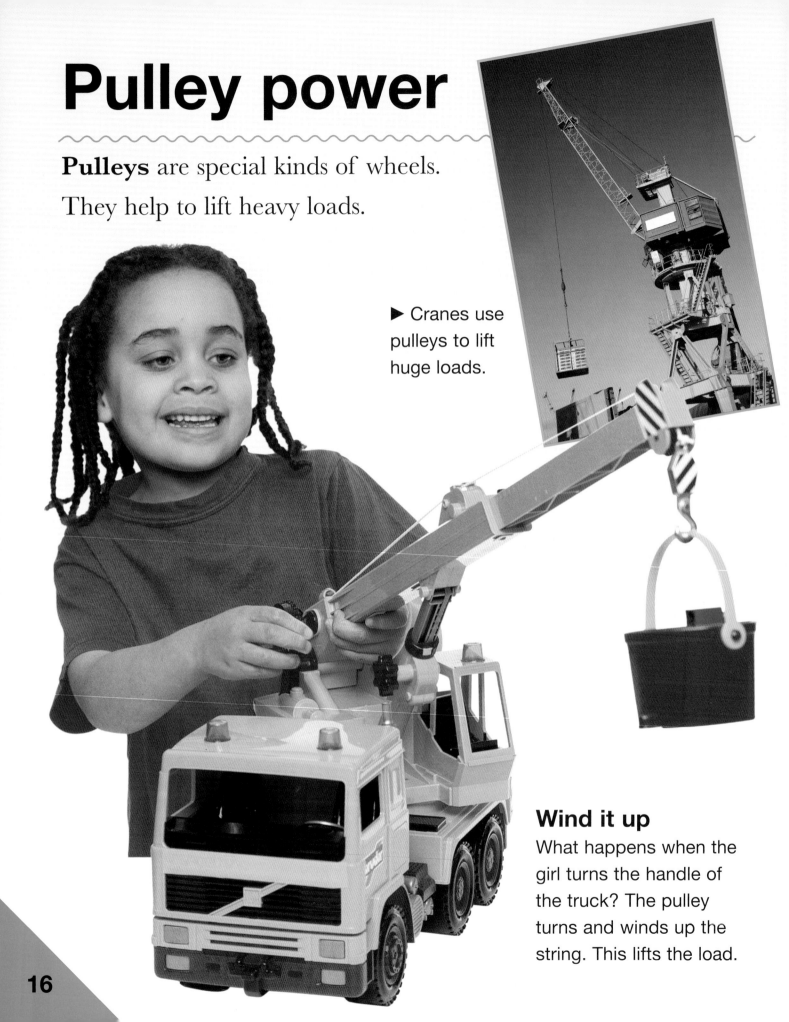

▶ Cranes use pulleys to lift huge loads.

Wind it up

What happens when the girl turns the handle of the truck? The pulley turns and winds up the string. This lifts the load.

Lift a load

You will need: two chairs, thin stick, sticky tape, toy bucket, toy bricks, empty cotton reel.

1 Tie a string to a toy bucket full of toy bricks. Now tape a stick between two chairs.

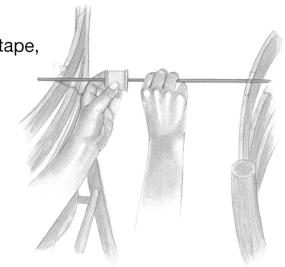

3 Push the stick through an empty cotton reel. Retape it to the chairs.

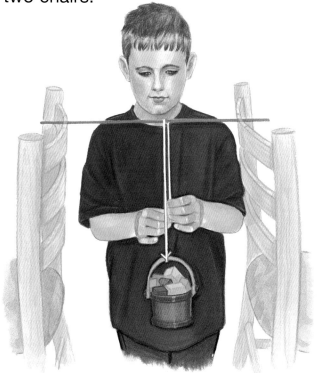

2 Pass the string over the stick. Pull on the string to lift the bucket.

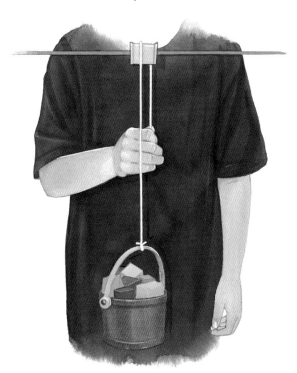

4 Pass the string over the reel and lift the bucket again.

Which bucket is easier to lift? It should be easier to lift the bucket with the cotton reel pulley.

Geared up

A **gear** is a special kind of toothed wheel. Gears help things turn and move easily.

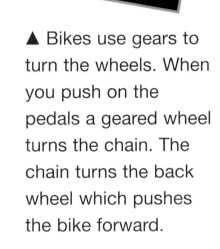

▲ Bikes use gears to turn the wheels. When you push on the pedals a geared wheel turns the chain. The chain turns the back wheel which pushes the bike forward.

Whisk it

Turn the handle of a whisk. Can you see how it turns the toothed wheels? These act as gears to turn the blades of the whisk.

Turning power

You will need: corrugated cardboard, round-ended scissors, eight cocktail sticks or toothpicks, two small corks, glue, two nails, thick piece of cork.

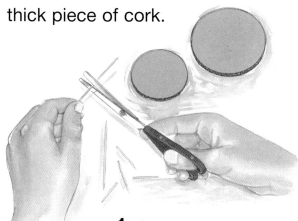

1 Cut out a large and a small circle from the cardboard. Cut eight cocktail sticks or toothpicks in half.

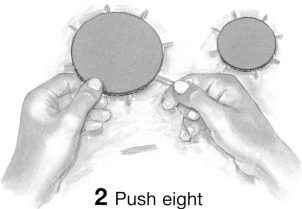

2 Push eight half-sticks evenly round each wheel.

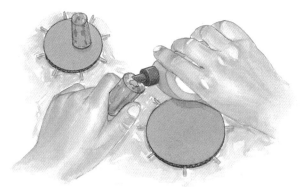

3 Stick a small cork near the edge of each wheel.

4 Push a nail through the middle of each wheel. Push the nails into a thick piece of cork. Make sure the stick 'teeth' on the wheels link together.

5 Turn the cork handle of one wheel. What happens to the other wheel?

The teeth lock together. They act as gears and both wheels turn.

Lifting loads

A **lever** is a bar that moves on a fixed point. When you push down on one end of a lever, the other end rises. We use levers to help lift heavy things.

Lift the lid

This lid is hard to get off. The woman is using a spoon as a lever. She has put one end of the spoon under the lid. She pushes down on the other end. This pushes up the end under the lid. The force of this push lifts off the lid.

Full force

You will need: bar of wood about 30cm/12in long, thin block of wood, small can.

1 Put a wooden bar, about 30cm/12in long, across a narrow block of wood. This is your lever.

2 Put a can at one end of the lever. Press down near the middle of the wooden bar. Can you lift the can?

Now press down at the end of the bar. Is the can easier to lift?

The lifting force is bigger the further away you push from the fixed point. The fixed point of your lever is where the bar rests on the block.

Levers at work

Find out how to make different kinds
of lever in these experiments.

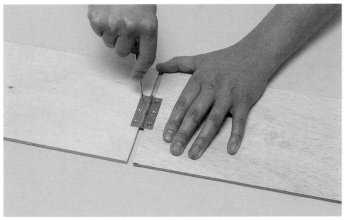

Can crusher

You will need: two short planks of wood
about 40 x 10cm/16 x 4in and 1–2cm/
½–¾in thick, hinge, screws, screwdriver,
two coffee-jar lids, glue, some empty
cans to crush.

1 Lay the two planks of wood end to end.
Ask an adult to help you screw them
together with a hinge, using screws and a
screwdriver. Make sure the hinge is secure.

2 Glue a jar lid to the inside edge of each plank
of wood, with the top of the lid face down. The
lids should be about halfway along each plank
and the same distance from the hinge.

3 To crush a can, place it in
between the lids, so that it is
held in place. Press down hard
on the top piece of wood.

Balance scale

You will need: thick cardboard 50 x 8cm/ 20 x 3in, thin cardboard, scissors, string, ruler, hole punch, 12cm/4½in circle of thin cardboard, tape, 100g/4oz of coins, felt-tipped pen, some objects to weigh.

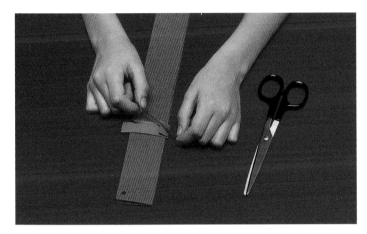

1 Make the arm by folding the thick cardboard in two. Make a loop of thin cardboard and fold it loosely around the arm 11cm/4¼in from one end. Tie a piece of string to this support.

2 Make a hole 1cm/½in from the arm's end. Make the cardboard circle into a cone. Tie it to the hole. Make an envelope from thin cardboard, and tie it to a loop so that it hangs over the arm.

3 Put the coins in the envelope and seal it up. Starting from the middle of the support, make a mark every 5cm/2in along the arm. This scale will tell you the weight of an object.

4 To weigh an object, put it in the cone and slide the envelope of coins backwards and forwards along the arm, until the arm balances. Each mark on the scale equals 50g/2oz. In this picture, the object being weighed is about 75g/3oz.

Balancing points

When things are balanced they do not tip over. They are held in balance by gravity. This balancing point is called the **centre of gravity.**

Bend over

Are you good at balancing? Try this.

Put a ball on the floor near a wall. Stand with your back to the wall. Your heels should be touching the wall. Now try to pick up the ball without moving your feet. What happens?

You can't do it! Your balance point moves forward as you bend over. So you have to move your feet to stop yourself falling over.

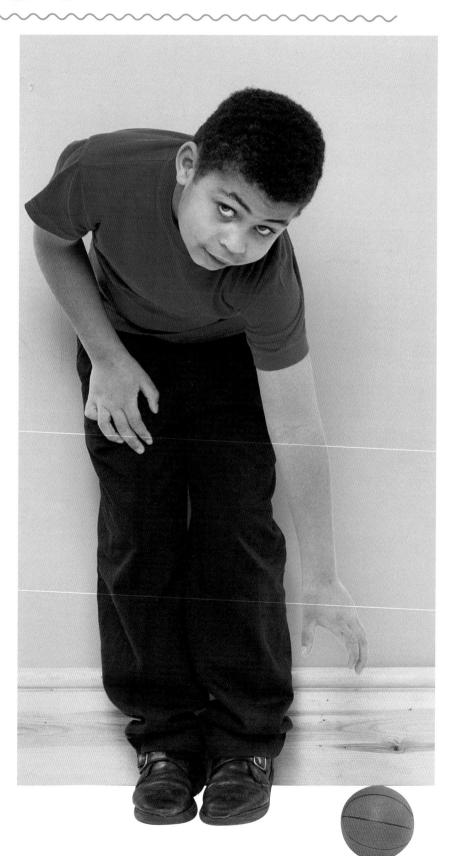

Star acrobat

You will need: cardboard, pencils in various shades, round-ended scissors, two coins, glue, thick string, two chairs.

1 Draw two doll shapes on cardboard (you could photocopy and enlarge these). Draw one doll as the front and the other as the back. Cut them out.

2 Fix a coin to the inside of each foot.

3 Glue the two halves of the doll together. Leave it to dry.

4 Stretch thick string tight between two chairs. Can you balance the doll on the string?

The weight of the coins keeps the doll's centre of gravity in its legs, so the doll should balance.

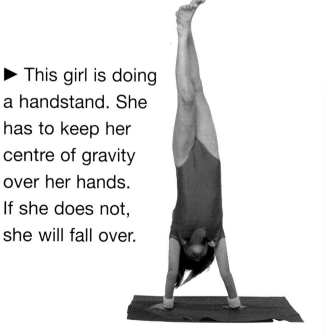

▶ This girl is doing a handstand. She has to keep her centre of gravity over her hands. If she does not, she will fall over.

Swinging by

Some machines use swinging movements to make them work. Let's find out about **pendulums**.

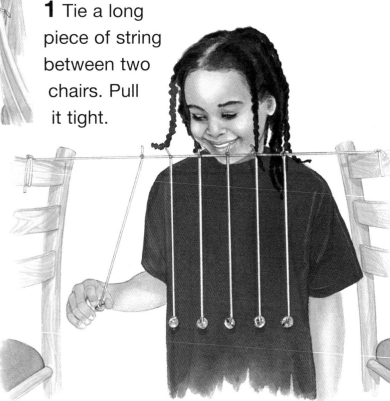

Move on

You will need: string, six marbles, sticky tape, two chairs (you may need two friends to sit on the chairs to keep them still).

1 Tie a long piece of string between two chairs. Pull it tight.

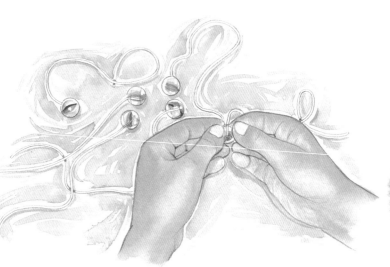

2 Cut six pieces of string, each 30cm/ 12in long. Tape a marble to each one. Tie the ends of the strings to your string line about 3cm/1in apart, ensuring that they are level.

3 Swing one marble to hit the next. What happens to the other marbles?

The first marble hits the second which hits the third and so on. The last marble swings out.

Back and forth

You will need: string, sticky tape, one large and one small plastic brick, a watch with a second hand.

1 Cut two pieces of string, 30cm/12in long. Tape a large plastic brick to one and a small brick to the other.

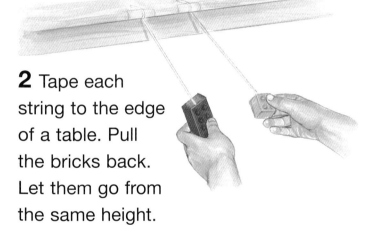

2 Tape each string to the edge of a table. Pull the bricks back. Let them go from the same height.

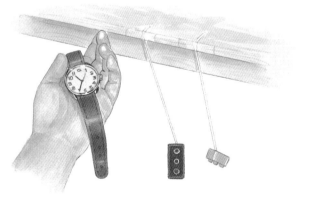

3 Time ten swings for each one. Do they take different times? The times should be the same for both bricks.

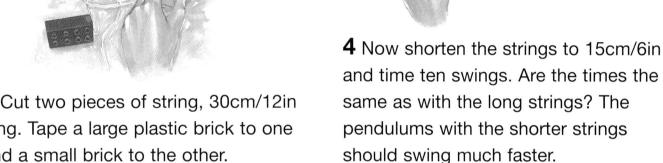

4 Now shorten the strings to 15cm/6in and time ten swings. Are the times the same as with the long strings? The pendulums with the shorter strings should swing much faster.

▼ Builders use a machine which swings a heavy ball on the end of a chain. This machine can knock down big buildings.

Wind and water power

Machines need energy to make them move. Most use petrol or electricity. Some use the pushing force of water or the wind.

Air power

1 Make a wheeled box car as shown on page 15. Ask a grown-up to cut out the end and top of the box.

▲ Wind turbines use the pushing force of the wind to make electricity.

You will need: wheeled box car from page 15, long-shaped balloon.

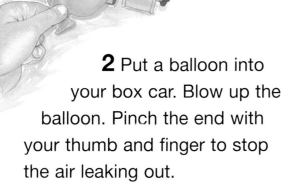

2 Put a balloon into your box car. Blow up the balloon. Pinch the end with your thumb and finger to stop the air leaking out.

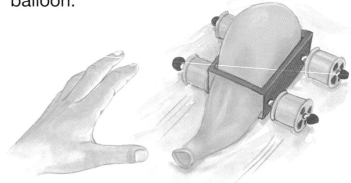

3 Let it go!
The air rushes out of the balloon. The force of the air moving backwards pushes the box car forwards.

Water power

Water wheels are used to move machinery and make electricity.

You will need: five small plastic pots, strong glue, empty cotton reel, thin round stick.

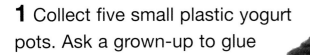

1 Collect five small plastic yogurt pots. Ask a grown-up to glue the pots round a cotton reel.

2 Push a thin, round stick through the middle of the cotton reel.

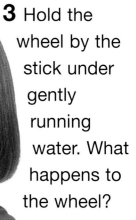

3 Hold the wheel by the stick under gently running water. What happens to the wheel?

The pushing force of the water should turn your wheel.

Hints to helpers

Pages 6 and 7

Explain that gravity holds most things to the surface of the Earth and stops them floating in the air. Discuss the fact that you use a lot of energy walking up a steep flight of stairs because you are fighting against gravity.

Explain how Earth's gravity makes falling objects speed up as they fall towards the ground. Their speed does not depend on their weight. The further the marble falls, the faster it is moving as it hits the sand. It hits the sand with a greater force and so the hole is deeper. Explain that, in order to make the test a fair one, the marble must just be let go, not thrown down.

Discuss what would happen to a soft object if it fell from different heights. Suggest the children drop a ball of non-hardening clay from different heights to see what happens to its shape.

Pages 8 and 9

Discuss the different types of forces, for example pulling, pushing and stretching, that the children can use to move an object or change its shape. Talk about whether a small pull or push uses more force than a big pull or push. Explain that the more they stretch a rubber band, the more force they are using.

This means that the distance the band has stretched can be used to see how much force is needed to move an object.

Discuss why it is important that, for the test to be fair, the tube must be at the same angle and that the ball should be allowed to roll down the tube, not pushed. Explain that gravity pulls the ball down the tube. Talk about how the pushing force of the ball as it hits the truck moves the truck forwards. The distance it moves depends on the pushing force and the truck's weight. The pushing force stays the same, so the loaded truck doesn't move as far as the empty truck.

Pages 10 and 11

Discuss how objects need a force both to start and to stop them moving. Friction is a force that stops movement. In the test, smooth objects move more easily because there is little friction between them and the wood.

Pages 12 and 13

Discuss how we can use friction to help us move and stop. For example, using the results of the test, discuss how we can increase friction to help us walk on icy ground. Talk about the best kinds of shoes to wear for different activities.

Pages 14 and 15

Discuss why it is easier to push or pull things up a gentle slope than up a steep one. Talk about why people use more energy, and get more tired, climbing a steep hill than a gentle one.

Discuss how the wheeled car has less of its surface in contact with the ground than the flat box. Talk about how this will reduce friction and so help the car to move. Discuss how the fact that the wheels turn, rather than drag, along the ground also reduces friction and helps the car to move so that less force is needed.

Pages 16 and 17

The pulley in the test is a single pulley. It allows you to lift a heavy load directly beneath the pulley more easily. You could try using two cotton reel pulleys (placing the sticks parallel to one another) as a double pulley. A double pulley needs much less pulling force to lift the same load. (N.B. a much longer piece of string will be needed.)

Pages 18 and 19

Look at how the wheels fit together in an egg whisk. Count how many times the small wheel turns when you turn the big wheel. Each time a larger wheel is turned, it can turn a smaller wheel several times. The number of times the small wheel turns depends on the number of cogs (teeth) each wheel has.

When you turn the big wheel, the teeth should lock and turn the small wheel. The small wheel turns faster. Try adding different numbers of teeth to each wheel. Try to find out which arrangement turns the small wheel the fastest.

Pages 20 and 21

Explain that using a lever is a simple way to lift heavy loads more easily. Levers increase the pushing force underneath an object, so a load can be moved with less effort. The further away the pushing power is from the fulcrum (fixed point), the less force is needed to lift the object. Try putting the can at different distances from the fulcrum to see what effect this has on the force needed to lift the can. Levers have greater power the nearer the object is to the fulcrum.

Pages 22 and 23

Explain that the balance scale is like the ones used by the ancient Romans. It works by balancing the weight of an object against a known weight, in this case a bag of coins. The coins are moved along the lever arm, until they balance the object being weighed. The farther away from the fulcrum the weighed bag is, the greater turning effect it has on the lever arm. The heavier the weight being measured, the farther away the bag must be moved to balance the arm. The weight is read against the scale along the arm.

Pages 24 and 25

Discuss how all objects have a point where they are held in balance by gravity. The balance point of a regular shape such as a square is its central point. Explain how objects with a low centre of gravity are less likely to topple over. In the doll, the weights in the legs keep the centre of gravity low down in the legs, so although more of the figure is above the string, the doll will balance.

Pages 26 and 27

Discuss how a pendulum needs a force to make it start moving. When a swinging pendulum hits another object, the pushing force is passed on. In the first test, the pushing force of the swinging movement is passed on as each marble hits the next one in line. The last marble should swing out as the pushing force of the previous marble hits it. As the last marble swings back, it will send the pushing force back down the line.

Talk about clocks that use pendulums to make them work. Emphasize the two things the children have learned from their tests. The weight on the end of a pendulum does not affect the time the pendulum takes to make one swing. However, the length of the string does affect the time the pendulum takes to make one swing.

Pages 28 and 29

Discuss the kinds of machines people use to move things more easily. Discuss how machines use energy and forces to make things move. Talk about how a child uses a bicycle to move more quickly. The energy to move the bicycle comes from the child pushing down on the pedals. This pushing power turns the wheels to move the bicycle. Discuss how natural forces, such as the pushing power of wind and water, can be used to turn wheels and work machines. Talk about why this may be better than using finite fuels such as petrol or coal to work machines.

Glossary

Centre of gravity The balance point of an object. When an object is balanced, it does not fall over. An object can balance more easily if it has a balance point near its base, or foot.

Force Something that changes the movement or shape of an object. For example, pushing, pulling, twisting, stretching and squashing are all different kinds of forces.

Friction A force that slows down or stops the movement of one surface over another. We use friction to slow things down. For example, brakes use friction to slow down a turning wheel. Friction makes heat and wastes energy. We can reduce friction by putting a layer of oil or grease between moving parts.

Gear A toothed wheel. Two or more gears can connect together to help things move. Gears can pass the movement of one set of wheels to another. Gears can be used to move different parts of a machine.

Gravity The force between two objects that pulls them together. It is what pulls all things towards the Earth.

Lever A simple machine made up of a bar that moves on a fixed point. Levers can be used to help lift heavy things.

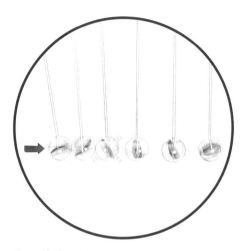

Pendulums
These are rods or strings which have a weight on one end. They swing backwards and forwards from a fixed point.

Pulleys Special wheels. A rope fits into a groove around the rim of the wheel. If the end of the rope is tied to a heavy object, the pulley helps you to lift the object more easily.

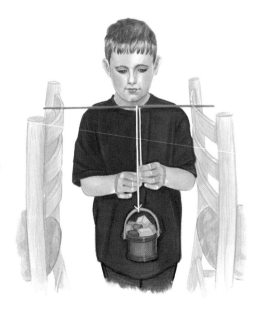